The Silent Songs of Butterflies

The Silent Songs of Butterflies

(Stories in Verse Both Light and Dark)

by David Reid

silentsongsofbutterflies.com

Cover art images used under license from:
Unholy Vault Designs / Shutterstock.com

ISBN 978-1-7771285-0-0 (paperback)
ISBN 978-1-7771285-1-7 (electronic book)

Thanks:

Putting Up With Me	- Cindy, My Love.
Challenging Me To Write	- Brittany M. and Alisha G.
Beta Reading, Ego Fluffing, Inspirational Art and Conversation	- Alisha G., - Brittany M. and - Courtney H.
Inspirational Absurdity	- Night shift and the Odder Parts of My Brain.

What Is This?

It's clearly not poetry.
It's verse - of a kind.
It's written in stanzas
And - usually - it rhymes.

I've laboured with meter
Though sometimes I've failed.
“Iambic,” it isn't.
It’s much more down-scale.

It's how that I passed
Some long hours at night.
When parts of my brain
Weren’t working quite right.

So, yes, it's an odd
Collection of verse,
A gamut of rhymings
- For whatever it's worth.

Contents

(An awful lot of blank pages.)

The Silent Songs of Butterflies

(Argh! Here's another one!)

A Candle Alight

There're some of us drawn to the darkness.
Of them I'm one, so I guess,
Safe with our lights of electric,
Fascinated by Pandora's Chest.
Still, I can't help but to wonder,
Inside - in that Land-Ever-Night -
Do the monsters there ever close gather
To stare at a candle alight?

*This coalesced one night while I was trying to fill my sleepless hours by coming up with a title for this collection. In the end, I chose a different title, but I kept the verse.

Newton

In a land
Beyond the sea,
Where wishes bloom
And dreams can be,
There lives a hoard
Of dragons there,
Those wondrous beasts
Of Flame and Air.

They make their home
Upon an isle,
Cloaked from human
Eyes by guile
And ring-ed round
With magic spells
That keep their land
All to themselves.

For, long ago,
They learned that "Man"
- With pointy sticks
And dressed like cans -
Would oft' oppose
A dragon's rest,
Considering it
A noble quest
To show themselves
Both brave and bold
By stealing dragons'
Gems and gold.

Avoiding Man
- Both dame and knight -
The dragons all
As one took flight,
Retired to
Those shores and sands
And built their homes
On warm, dry land.

For, freed at last
From threat of thieves,
Their scaly skins
Were much relieved
To dwell up in
The sun's bright rays
And ne'er again
In cold, damp caves.

And, so they wouldn't
Be alone,
They built a town
Of brick and stone,
Clustered close
In threes and twos
And painted bright
In gemstone hues.

In Sol's gold light,
The hamlet glowed
- So much so,
They called it "Trove,"
A beacon to
The Dracan race
That called out, "*Home*
Is *here*. *This* place."

Soon every drake,
Though seas apart,
Felt its tug
Upon their heart
And made their way
To its warm shore.
They came in twos
And tens and scores
'Til their village
Was a town
And then a city
Far renowned.

There, Dragon lore
And culture prospered
With music, wit
And learning fostered.
- Though all *these* things
Did pale beside
The things that swelled
Their hearts with pride.

For Dracan cunning
- Which Men held legend -
In Dragons' tales,
Was seldom mentioned.
While subtle arts
Were viewed as pleasures,
'Twas brutal traits
They truly *treasured.*

Bulk and brawn
And strength and speed,
These the things
That *dragons* heed,
Hotter flame
And harder scales,
Louder roars
And longer tails.

And when young dragons
Got together,
They were not ones
To chat of weather.
They spun tall tales
Of epic flights,
Of made-up quests,
And fearsome fights.
And by and by
This too oft' led
To all too real blows
To their heads.

So wiser drakes
- The ancient ones -
Said "Come now, hatchlings,
Let's have some fun.
You want to settle
Who's the best?
Don't stand around
And beat your chests.
We'll organize
A set of games -
A flying race,
A test of flame,
Measurements
Of widths and lengths,
Displays of toughness,
Feats of strength."

And so were hatchling
Passions leashed
And - under written
Rules - released.
Referees
Were duly named
And thus was birthed:
The Dracan Games.

A right of passage
Now are the Games
For dragons old
Enough to flame.
For 'ere a "hatchling"
Can reach "drake,"
They must the Dracan
Games partake.

The first event
Is always "Flame"
For this is how
They earn their name.
By breathing fire,
They come of age
And that is how
Their worth is gauged.
- Those who cannot
Make a burn
Are deemed not "drake,"
But lesser "wyrm."

Once Trial Of Fire
Is then behind them,
Rules of Hatchlings
No longer bind them.
They are then free
To make their claims
And prove them in
The Dracan Games.

To this world
Was Newton born.
…Well, more like "hatched"
- As was their norm.
First of clutch
To burst from egg,
Newton was green
As a parent could beg.

His scales were all shiny,
His fangs deadly sharp,
His neck long and writhe-y,
His wings tough as tarp.
Yes, Newton, the hatchling,
Was the cause of much braggin',
The "Treasure of Trove"
And of *all* of its dragons.

With finest of scales
And sharpest of teeth,
Straight from his shell
He accomplished great feats.
He sprang to the sky
On still drying wings
And teased all the terns
By nipping their wings.
He out-wheeled the gulls
Over fields lying fallow
And out-roared the surf
As it surged through the shallows.

There were great expectations
For Newton, the hatchling.
He grew like a weed
And no one could match him.
The next time the Games
Could be held on the isle,
Surely, he'd triumph
And do so with style!

The whole of the city
Could scarce wait for the Games,
For Newton, the *Dragon*,
To win and be named
The biggest, the fastest
With hottest of fire.
But, alas, something happened
- And it turned out quite dire.
He developed a syndrome
- A stomach complaint -
That stunted his growth
And peeled walls of their paint.

He'd feel a great gurgle
Deep down in his tum
To and then through
To his il-eum.
Inch by inch,
It would make its progression,
The churning gases
Of digestion,
'Til - pressure rising
In the bowel -
It vented out
A scent most foul.

At first, all his peeps,
They all stood by fast.
This odd, passing thing,
Without doubt, couldn't last.
Their hero would soon
Be right as the rain
And then just bring on
The Grand Dracan Games!

But Newton himself
Was not quite so sure
And he worried about it
More and then more.
And, the more that he worried,
The worse grew the cramp
'Til, sooner than later,
It burst through the clamp
That he'd put on his bum
To hold it all in.
And, when it let loose,
It made quite a din.

It rolled and it echoed
In thunderous proportions
With the stench of the blast
Causing facial contortions
In any living thing
Unfortunately near
Whose eyes would then redden
And fill up with tears.

Like leaves in the autumn,
Newt began to lose fans
'Til finally, when they spied him,
Most dragons just ran.
"Sorry," they'd say
To the breeze as they fled,
"But the odour from you
Is too much like the dead."

Yes, fame is quite fickle
- Especially when gratis –
And slowly, but surely,
Newt lost social status.
No longer "Trove's Treasure,"
He fell out of favour.
Yesterday's hero
Was now yesterday's flavour.

Oh, they'd give him the time
Of the day - if he asked -
But the era of "Newton,
The Hero" was past.
No longer the treasure
That had caused all the buzzin',
Just one of the crowd
- One, among dozens.

Farther and farther
Newt lagged all his peers.
'Twas worse than he'd worried,
Far worse than he'd feared.
While the rest of his clutch
Continued to grow,
Newton's dimensions
Were sadly plateaued.
At the next Dracan Games,
It began to look dim
That he'd even take part
- Let alone that he'd win.

But the Trial of Flame,
That was his *right*.
He'd earn him his place
By blazing up bright.
He may not be the biggest,
- No matter how he yearned -
But he'd be a true dragon
And not just some *wyrm*.

He might not be the *victor*
Of the next Dracan Games,
But he vowed he'd breath fire,
That he'd earn a good name,
Like "Newt, the Inferno"
Or "Newton, the Blaze"
...Or even just "Sparky"
For at least, 'twas a Name.

At last, came the day.
The Games were at hand.
They unfurled the banners
And struck up the bands.
They called all the hatchlings
To line up in queue
To show all the ancients
What the new kids could do.

A big, yellow dragon
Walked up to their line,
"Don't worry, hatchlings.
I'm sure you'll do fine.
Set your sharp claws
Down there in the earth,
Then push your breath forth
For all that you're worth.
Blow out all the gas
Hard from your chest.
The magic of chemistry
Will do all the rest."

And here their drake mentor
Grew greatly excited,
"Your breath is the fuel.
The air will ignite it!
Just take a deep breath,
Then focus your thought.
Keep holding it in
As you feel it grow hot.
Then hold it some more
- You *can* if you try -
And, just when you feel
The tears well in your eyes,
Let it all loose.
Push with all of your might.
Send it all forth
And let it burn bright!
If you be true dragons,
Your flame will burn hot.
For those masquerading,
...Alas, it will not."

Then the big drake
Looked at each of their faces
As if looking for flaws
Or even small traces.
But he broke to a grin
And he said, "Not to fear.
I'm sure that won't happen
To anyone here.
A finer a brood
I don't think I've seen,
Rougher and tougher
And really quite keen.
Now, who'll be the first?
Who'll make the first claim?
Who'll win the first entry
To this year's Grand Games?"

The first to the line
Was a bronze named J'Loo
From a long line of dragons
Both noble and true.
He huffed and he puffed,
Then he blew it all forth
And it lit up bright orange
In a great jetting torch.

“Not bad for first try,
But there’re lots to go yet.
Congrats there, young dragon,
Now named - 'J’Loo Jet.'
That’s how it’s done kids!
J’Loo showed the way,”
Said their big, yellow mentor.
“Now, who’s next to the fray?”

One by one, the salamanders
Walked up to the line,
Nervous, but hopeful
That they’d get the sign
That they were approved,
That they’d earned rank and name,
That they now could enter
The rest of the Games.

Just as the ref said,
That year, a good crop.
All had made flame
And none had made not.
Most certainly, yes,
The best in long years
And with each new success
The watching crowd cheered.

The Trial carried on
'Til there was only one left,
Only one hopeful
To still take the test.
“Come along, Newton,”
Said the big, dragon coach.
“Now, don’t be so nervous.
You’re as pale as a ghost.”

But Newton *was* nervous
And his legs were like jelly
For he was feeling *that* feeling
Way down in his belly.
But if he was quick,
Yes, if he was fast,
He’d finish his trial
Before the knot (um) ...passed.

So that’s what he did,
Looked not left and not right.
He stepped to the plate,
Drew breath, held it tight.
Just like the coach said,
He’d wait for the burn
- Then horror of horrors! -
He felt his guts churn.

He felt a great gurgle
Deep down in his tum
To and then through
To his il-eum.
Inch by inch,
It made its progression.
The churning gases
Of digestion
Went coursing through
His rectum fast,
Then jetted out
In one great *blast*!

One far off cricket
Then drown out the crowd
'Til finally there came
One voice - and quite loud -
"I can't see what happened.
Did he fail? Or have luck?
And what was that sound?
- Someone step on a duck?"
The crowd roared with laughter.
Poor Newton was crushed.
He hung his head lowly.
He reddened and blushed.

"Hey... Hey..." growled the judges.
"Let's have none of that,"
Then they went to poor Newton
And they gave him a pat.
"It's okay there, young Newt.
A 'misfire' that's all.
Flame *oft'* doesn't answer
The *first* time it's called.
Go back to your place
And have one more go.
And when it feels right,
We're sure that you'll know."

Swallowing hard,
Newt went back to the line,
Waited for the moment
When he felt it was time,
Then took a deep breath
And he screwed his eyes shut
- And a great gout of flame
Shot straight out his butt!

The fuel in air,
Had self combusted.
Rudely forward,
Newt was thrusted!
Braced as he was
For a jolt from the front,
The kick from behind
Gave him quite a bunt.
Newt stumbled forward,
A disastrous lurch
That ended up planting
His face in the dirt
And as he lay there
Fig'ring out what had happened,
He noted a silence
That grew and then fattened.

The crowd all around
Was as still as a tomb.
The sound of a pin-drop
Would have made a great boom.
A marvelous muffle,
Where not a leaf stirred
And no one dared swallow
For fear it be heard.
A soft, fluffy blanket,
Both thick and profound.
You could hear shadows whisper
And the sun beating down.
Yes, the quiet created
Was dense and complete
As all in the crowd
Seemed to study their feet.

None knew what to say,
Nor just what to think
As the awful, awkward silence
Hung there like stink.
Newton moved not a muscle.
All hope was now past.
Not dragon, just wyrm.
His lot had been cast.

At last, the big drake
Took the bull by the horns
And, clearing his throat,
“Most unusual form,
But none can deny
That, yes, you’ve made flame.
You’re one of us now,
So ‘Welcome’ to the Games.”

Newton’s heart soared
To hear this decision,
But there in the crowd
Sounded notes of derision.
“We’ve heard of discretion,
But this is a farce!
A dragon whose head
Is disguised as his *arse*?
Come off of it, R’oy.
Have you been struck blind?
Flame shoots out front
And not from behind.”

But R'oy was quite stubborn
And wouldn't back down.
Standing up to the rabble,
He said, "Look here, you clowns.
Newt's stood the Great Trial
And *I* say he's won.
I've made my decision.
It's final and *done*."

Back and then forth,
The argument swayed,
But neither side softened
And neither side gave,
While poor Newton wished
He could just disappear
Or - failing that magic -
To be anywhere but here.

But stuck there he was
As debate grew more heated
And all the long while
The day's hours retreated.
It soon wouldn't matter
How the squabble turned out.
For, the Games, they went on
With Newt or without.

Then, through the crowd,
Flowed a great silver queen
Saying "Pardon me, R'oy,
But I'm sure we've all seen
That our dearest, young Newton
Did indeed pass the Trial,
- With the *most* stylish flair
That I've seen in some while.
I support your decision.
Now let this tiff end.
Be off with you, Newton.
You've no time to spend."

Just like that, it was done
And there'd be no dissent
For the word of a "Silver"
Was as high as it went.
- They were the wisest
And the greatest of hues
And, whenever they spoke,
You gave them their due.
No mumbles, no grumbles,
No "yes, buts" or "maybes."
You just did what they asked,
And said "Thank you, Great Lady."

And so it was now
That she'd made this decree.
All question was ended
And all now agreed.
"Newton, the Hatchling,"
Was now "Newton, the Dragon,"
And all that remained was
The Official Name-Taggin'.

"What, then, shall we name him?"
Big Yellow R'oy asked,
"The Games are soon ending,
So think one up fast."
Then a voice from the crowd
- One of those from the back -
Said "How 'bout 'Tootin' Newton'?"
And every one laughed.

But to the shock of them all,
The judge said "Okay.
'Tootin' Newton' hurry off
- And good luck this day."
Amid smiles and chuckles,
The crowd soon dispersed
And now, all alone,
Newt could hardly feel worse.

But, no, *not* alone
For there, still, was the queen,
The most beautiful dragon
Newt had e'er seen.
She leaned down to him now
Saying "Newton, don't worry.
Go win at the Games.
You've a chance if you hurry.
All the others are over,
There's just one test remaining,
The Fast Flying Trial,
So you'll *not* be abstaining.
It's the one chance you've got
To re-write your name.
The Games are soon ending,
So go now. Find fame!"

Newton opened his mouth
To say "Thank you, your Grace,"
But, before he could speak,
She said, "Go now. Make haste!"

Now, “bigger” and “stronger”
And “louder” were things
All worthy of bragging,
But “fastest” was *king*!
It out-trumped the others
And gave highest ranking
And, in each of their hearts,
Each young dragon was banking
That *they*’d win “The Race”
And be 'ever known
As the swiftest of flyers,
High above all the drones.

And Newt was no different.
In his heart, he still dreamed
That - in spite of his size -
He could still reign supreme,
That he’d win the Great Race
Though the odds stacked against him.
His digestive compliant?
He’d *not* let it bench him.

So, away Newton flew
To the site of the race
And arrived as the others
Were all taking their place.
They formed up a wedge
With point facing front
Led by the largest,
Then, following, the runts.
But no one complained
Or called it unfair.
'Twas the way that it was.
...They were (just) glad to be there.

Newton was shuffled
To the rear of the group,
So far in the back
That it made his wings droop.
As he looked all around,
All he saw were big bums
That towered above him
And blocked out the sun.

How could he ever
Even hope to compete,
Let alone win
- That would be quite a feat -
Placed as he was
At the back of the scrum?
Newt grew discouraged,
But then came "The *Drum*!"

'Twas the great kettle drum
That warned of the start
And each of its boomings
Plucked a string in Newt's heart.
The rush of great wings,
As each row released,
Soon drown out the drum
As the wedge, piece by piece,
Took to the air
And made for the sky
For the title of "Fastest
Of the Games" that they vied.

Newt's heart pounded fiercely
For his chance at the sky,
For his row to be signaled,
For *his* chance to fly.
He waited and waited.
Would his turn ever come?
His wings again sagging,
His outlook turned glum.

Then, all at once,
Bums began wiggling.
The row to his front
Was getting its signaling!
They sprang straight aloft,
Then Newton could see
That *his* turn was next
And his heart filled with glee!

The next beat of the drum
- Yes, again he could hear it -
Would signal *his* turn.
Now he was near it!
And then it *did* sound
And Newton was gone,
Last in the wedge,
But the race was now on!

Newton flew like an arrow,
Then he jinked and he wheeled
Around slower dragons
As he made up the field.
He was small, but was nimble
And maneuvered quite quick
In the sky that was crowded
With dragons so thick.

At the head of them all,
Newton soon flew,
Leading the pack
In a sky of bright blue.
But our hero soon found
That leaders have woes
As belligerent breezes
Against him arose.

They did buffet him soundly
And pushed him far back,
Back through the rankings
To the rear of the pack.
The others, much bigger,
Noticed not this slight zephyr,
But to Newt, it was wild,
A hurricane to his "feather."

His furious wings
Hummed like a bird's,
Faster and faster,
Disappeared in a blur.
But no matter his effort,
Newt steadily lost ground
To the bigger contestants
In his quest for the crown.

He flapped his wings hard
With all of his might,
But slowly the pack
Was lost to his sight.
They pulled away more,
Grew far and grew small
'Til Newton, our hero,
Could scarce see them at all.

He’d tried his most best,
But just could not do.
No way he could win,
Still, onward, he flew.
He’d be all alone
And, to that, grew resigned.
No trophies, no ribbons
For the last in the line.
No winner’s wreath
For the last in the race.
He’d lost his last chance
For saving his face.
Now he’d be his whole life,
He’d forever be named
“Rootin’ Tootin’ Newton
Of the Backward Aimed Flame.”
And the more that he thought,
The more that he worried
'Til there in his guts
He felt the old slurry.

He felt the great gurgle
Deep down in his tum
To and then through
To his il-eum.
Inch by inch,
It made its progression,
The churning gases
Of digestion,
'Til all at once
It burst the dam.
It hit the air
And then went BLAM!

Once more the fuel
Had self ignited
- With ten foot flame,
No hope to hide it.
But, there in the sky,
"Thrust" had its effect
And Newton took off
Just like a jet!

Action / reaction,
Hard acceleration,
Newton went zooming.
He felt joy and elation.
He ripped through the sky,
A great blazing comet
Worthy of legends,
Of sagas, of sonnets.

As his speed petered out
And lost its great surge,
Newt once again focused,
Concentrated, then "purged."
He had hang of it now.
He'd just meter it out.
Now comprehending,
He was back on his route.
Soon Newton could sec
The pack up ahead,
No longer bunched up,
But strung out like a thread.

Afterburner ablaze,
- If you take my meaning -
To the head of the line,
Newton went speeding.
He caught, then he passed,
First one, then another,
Then, clear sky ahead,
Opened up on his gov'nor.

At the Great Race's finish,
Where an eager crowd waited,
There was heard, in the distance,
A sound much debated.
It was far off, but growing
And it buzzed like a bee,
But from where it was coming
...Well, no one could see.

There was smoke in the distance
And a bright pulsing light.
Could it be the young racers?
Or were they still out of sight?
And yet there was something
In the sound quite familiar,
Like the blare of a trumpet
Only muffled and sillier.
What could it be?
Oh, what *could* it be?
It was still coming fast
So, soon, they would see.

The cloud of smoke grew and,
As it did, it resolved
To the cluster of racers.
- That was one mystery solved -
But what of the light
That still pulsed on and off
At the head of the pack
And that made that strange cough?

Soon questions were answered
As Newton's jet roared,
Rounding the finish
To claim his reward.
Touching down on the circle,
He stood on the turf.
Newton beamed in his victory
'Til his heart nearly burst.

But no checkered flag
Could be seen nearby waving.
And where was the trophy
With his name in engraving?
Newton looked 'round.
What was the matter?
Then he saw the Race-Jury
To one side tightly gathered.

They huddled up closely
From the eavesdropping crowd
And they murmured and puzzled
Over what was allowed.
"Was it fair to deploy
Jet powered enhancement
To augment one's flight
In pursuit of advancement?
What would be next?
Sails and propellers?
We must draw the line here,
...No offense, li'l feller."

"A most noble effort
And quite innovative,
But 'flight' tests our skill,
Our strength and things native."

"But the passing of wind,"
Someone else seized the thread,
"*Is* natural to Newton.
- Though our noses may dread -
I say if it's nature
Then it *should* be allowed."
And sounds of agreement
Were heard in the crowd
And there, at the back,
Once again, was the Queen
Who nodded her head
Saying "So let it be."

"Newton," she continued,
"It's my duty and right
To now give you a name
That honours your flight.
No more 'Tootin' Newton,'
But a name with more class.
I dub thee now 'Newton,
The Fiery Flash.'"

A good name, a strong name
And one with much favour.
Newton now had
A name to be savoured.
He smiled a tired "Thanks"
And then he collapsed,
Finally, decidedly,
For once ...out of gas.

*When I wrote this, I had just finished a series of verse stories starring a dragon named J'Loo. In case you missed it, he was the first of the hatchlings to make flame.

The Monster in My Room

“Mommy! There’s a monster
Underneath my bed!
I hear his tummy growling
And I think he wants me dead!”

Mother opened up one eye
To view her darling son
Still red-faced and panting
From his hallway run.

“Junior, you should know by now
That’s just the purr of 'Kitty'.
She sleeps down there beneath your bed
And she’s just itty-bitty.

Big Boys like you should not be scared
Of little kitty-cats.
So back to bed. Don’t be afraid.
You’re much too old for that.”

“Mommy! There's a monster
And he’s running 'round my room!
He’s running, Mommy! Very fast!
'Round and 'round! Va-room!”

Mother opened up one eye
Within her mudpack mask
And took a breath to swallow down
Some words that might seem rash.

"Junior, you should know by now
The fan out in your hall
That spins around the ceiling light
Casts shadows on your walls.

Big Boys like you should not be scared
Of a little shadow.
So back to bed. Don't be afraid.
Off you go. Skedaddle."

"Mommy! There's a monster
And he's hiding in my closet!
He's big and blue! And scary too!
In my room! I saws it!"

Mother opened up one eye
More bloodshot than before
To see her eldest offspring
Come sprinting through her door.

Then she sat up straight in bed
And gave a mighty shout,
"Enough of this! Get back to bed!
From my room, get OUT!"

He sat there in the hallway
And he tried to dry his eyes.
He sat outside his bedroom door
Too scared to go inside.

Submerged within his pity,
Poor Junior didn't hear
The softly padding footfalls
Until they grew quite near.

When all at once he heard them,
He spun himself around
To find his little sister
There in her dressing gown.

Little Sister, young but wise,
Only three years aged,
Held a box of crayons
And a clean, white page.

"When I's a monster in my room,
In my room's dark closet,
I gets my bestest crayons and
I sits right down and draws it.
I gives it sharp and curly horns
And a jillion eyes.
I 'xaggerate a little bit
And draws it twice its size.
When I'm done my pi'ture,
I takes it to my room
And shows it to the monster
And then he's gone. Ka-Boom!
He gets afraid and runs away
And don't come back again.
He don't like his ugly face
And that's the last of him."

She handed him her crayon box
And the clean, white sheet
And sat and watched her brother draw
Until he was complete.

A fearsome fiend indeed now dwelled
Upon the sheet of paper
And so they went to Junior's room
To turn the beast to vapour.

They cracked the door into his room,
Then he said, “You wait here
'Cause I’m a 'Big Boy' strong and brave
And I have naught to fear.
But you are just a little girl,
Not much more than a baby.
No, it’s best if you wait here
While I go show my bravery.”

So, as she waited in the hall,
Big Brother went on in.
She waited and she waited,
But did not see him again.

Fin-al-ly, she’d had enough.
She could wait no more,
So she took a big, deep breath
And pushed upon the door.

The door swung slow into the room
With a ghastly creak.
She stepped inside to look around
And took a furtive peek.

“Big Brother, are you in here?”
She asked the empty room,
But only silence answered
- And the soft light of the moon.

She listened to the silence
And she heard no kitty purr.
She looked upon the painted walls
And saw no shadows whir.

She looked then to the closet door
And saw it gaping wide,
Tip-toed 'cross the carpet
And took a look inside.

There the monster sat relaxed,
Toothpick in his hand.
He saw the girl. He smiled and said,
“A tasty, little man.
He walked in proud and straight and tall,
Right into my reach.
Such a juicy morsel,
Just like a lush, ripe peach!
Thank you, Miss. I must admit
Your plan worked to a tee.
Now I’ll consent to grant a wish
Just as we did agree.”

Standing in her PJs,
So cuddly and so sweet,
A greedy grin enwrapped her face
To show what lay beneath.

“Oh, that’s okay,” the wee lass said,
“I no more need your boon.
Now that Brother is gone at last,
Finally, I can have his room.”

The Raven's Call

The ebon bird, / the Raven, stands
Among the limbs / whose rigored hands
Beseech the skies / they could not reach.
Their time of life / long since complete.

In silence wait / the bleaching bones,
Now honoured as / the Raven's throne.
The Monarch laughs / and blinks an eye
For mortal things / that grow then die.

A bitter rasp, / the King then flies
To spread his call / across the skies,
"Ragnarok! / The world is done!"
So say the cries / of Raven's tongue.

His shadow finds / a single soul
Who now plays out / his destined role,
Dogged-ly / reciting names
Of comrades who / have failed their claim.
"Invincible" / – or so they thought –
Until the flame / of Ragnarok.

Like chaff they lie / upon the fields,
Their breath now stilled, / their blood congealed,
Remembered by / this single man
Whose life spills out / upon the sands.
The Raven wheels / and blinks an eye.
The Raven calls, / then windward flies.

A single rider / on the plain
For which now, / the Raven aims
And circles low / upon a quest
To peer upon / the face of Death.

The Horseman rides / a steed most pale
And at his back, / a mournful gale
Of souls enmeshed: / a Chorus Damned,
A last lament / for wasted lands.

The rider reins / and turns aside
And with him flows / the ghastly tide
Until they reach / that last live man
Still chanting out / his kith and clan.

"I know thee Death / as you know me
And with thee soon, / I know I'll be,
But while I live, / my kin remain
- As long as I / recall their names."

The man resumes / his task of naming
As his stuff / of life is draining.
'Neath the empty / gaze of Death,
The man remembers / less, then less
'Til only one name / does he speak.
His pulse grows thin, / his voice grows weak.
Still, he clings / to every breath
That gurgles now / inside his chest.
The Horseman waits, / still and silent,
His Cloak of Souls / commanded quiet,
'Til at last / the man's breath rattles.
The Grim One leaps / from pale mount's saddle.

The man is raised / in Death's strong arms,
Who - though he could - / does him no harm,
But keeps him close / and cradled dear,
Beyond all pain, / beyond all fear.

The Reaper's hand / then slips the clasp
Which holds the Cloak / upon Death's back
And swirls the cowl / and cape around
Until the man / within is bound.

The man awakes / within Death's Cloak,
Renewed and healed / within its yoke
And at his feet, / a pile of bones
As weathered as / the ancient stones.

The Raven calls, / decrees the time.
The Rider mounts / and gives the sign.
The bird then wheels / and glides the wind,
"Ragnarok! / The world begins!"

*From the old saying that "We're never truly gone until there's no one left to speak our name."

Extroverts

Extroverts are such big jerks.
They argue infinitum.
I wish King Kong would come along
And pick them up and bite them.

So busy spewing forth their brains,
They never listen fully.
Defensive offense in a chain.
They're great big, "sound bite" bullies.

They challenge all my careful words
Before I even say them
And place their thumbs upon my thoughts
Before I even weigh them.

They're big and loud and made of sound.
Their ears don't work too well.
They fart their words like loosened turds.
God damn them all to Hell.

*Obviously, I am a hardcore *in*trovert.

The Class of ‘05

As they put on / their hats / with their tassels,
There’s a gown / that’s draped over / one chair
Held reserved / for a girl / in a castle,
For a girl / with the Sun / in her hair.
Her sister / grown into / a woman.
Her brother / become / a young man.
Yet still, / she sleeps / as a child
Cradled safe / from Time’s / reaching hand.

In an album / we treasure / the pictures
- Precious moments / that are frozen / in time -
Of her face / in the joy / of her laughter,
Lit / from within / by her smile.

Her friends learn / to trifle / at “Sweethearts,”
Earn their share / of Love’s / little scars,
But none will / ever sting them / so badly
As the space / that she left / in their hearts.

It’s a place / that is silent / inside them
And it’s empty / except for / the girl.
They will visit / this place / and she’ll guide them
As they take up / the weight / of their worlds.

The heights of / their joys / are now bounded
By the grey / of the day / she was lost,
By the winds / and the waters / they mounded,
By the gift / of their lives / and its cost.

We may measure / the *length* / of her lifetime,
But we treasure / its *worth* / as a song,
In the gift / of her words / as she sang them,
In the joy / of their tune / echoed on.

In an album / we treasure / the pictures
- Precious moments / that are frozen / in time -
Of her face / in the joy / of her laughter,
Lit / from within / by her smile.

*Laurence Binyon beat me to it, but "They shall not grow old..."

Poop-a-pol-ooza

Haley with the blue eyes has a rumble in her tum.
Look out gals, she's gotta run.
She feels her belly gurgle and a pressure down below.
Look out! She has to go!

She bought some Pico-Salax and she drank it down
To get her ready for the short, blue gown.
No need to worry. It'll all be fine.
Gonna put a little camera where the sun don't shine.

Poop-a-pol-ooza, Poop-a-pol-ooza.
She can't come to the phone. She's sitting on the throne.
When will she be empty?

Sittin' on the toilet purging out her guts
Has left a reddened ring around her butt.
When the spasm's over and the chamber's spent,
She sits and she wonders where her breakfast went.

There's lots of heavy traffic on the Hershey Road.
All of it headin' to the white commode.
She's goin' and it's a flowin' like a garden hose.
She'd better flush it down so it don't overflow.

Poop-a-pol-ooza, Poop-a-pol-ooza.
Wouldn't it be sweet to have a padded seat?
When will she be empty?

Haley with the blue eyes has a rash upon her bum,
But we know where that it comes from.
The bargain toilet paper, it may save a bit of cash,
But it takes a frightful toll upon one's ass.

Swearing like a Frenchman, it would be so mighty fine
To the chafing parts back there behind.
Bet she'd spend some money for the use of a bidet
To make the burning fire go away.

Poop-a-pol-ooza, Poop-a-pol-ooza.
Now her bathroom warm sounds like a thunderstorm.
When will she be empty?

She's clean as a whistle in every cavity.
Peek for yourself and you'll agree.
All along the route that the camera took.
Log on to YouTube and take a look.

Poop-a-pol-ooza, Poop-a-pol-ooza.
You had to write a song? How long can this go on?
When will she be empty?

Haley with the blue eyes has a rumble in her tum.
Look out gals, she's gotta run.
She feels her belly gurgle and a pressure down below.
Look out! She has to GO!

*To the (approximate) tune of Raffi's "Baby Beluga".

Silence

Of Silence-built / my castle.
Of Stillness-hewn / each stone.
And there inside / do I reside
Upon my quiet throne.

Within I look / to see without.
I still my heart / and breath
To hear the horde / hung 'round my walls,
Their damn-ed din grotesque.

They come to fill / my peace with ill.
It's something / they abhor.
"Let them come," / my Silence hums,
"Just as they have before."

One speaks a word / to forward surge
The hungry beast / to break
In silent howls / from emptied bowels
Upon my soundless gate.

Their bodies crushed / within the rush,
By comrades / from behind...
Against my walls.... / The Silence falls.
Its stoic stones are blind.

And then the siege / begins again.
Great engines / built for war
To hurl their hatred / through the air,
A deadly rain to pour.

They strike my walls / without a sound…
'Til Silence / rolls like thunder,
Then, as it spreads, / the air turns dead
To tear the host asunder.

They race like ants / in frantic dance
To flee the / Silence growing,
But each in turn / is touched and burned
To silent ash unknowing.

Their refuse settles / slow and thick
Around my / still stone walls.
A blanket bound / unto the ground,
The last grey flake soon falls.

Of Silence-built / my castle.
Of Stillness-hewn / each stone.
And there inside / do I reside
Upon my quiet throne.

* The introvert's instinctive means of defense. Don't respond. It only energizes your antagonist.

The Tea Lion

As I sipped
My cup of tea,
I peered inside
For what I'd see
And there beheld
A Lion's Pride,
A golden mane
Flung full and wide.
And in that mane,
A Hunter's face,
Regal, strong
And full of grace.
Tables turned now,
He *my* prey,
The King inside
The last Earl Grey.
All he lacked
Were jewels and crown.
I pondered that...
Then drank him down.

* Prompted by a water colour lion, done using tea as the pigment.

Them Old Rollin' Bones

Them old rollin' bones,
They tumble and they fall.
They have led me past traps
That were laid in the walls.
They have spared me from spells
And from trolls ten feet tall.
They've preserved me from perils
In dark dungeon halls.

Them old rollin' bones,
They have helped me to find
Treasures of gold
And of all other kinds.
They have helped me to walk
Where no angel will tread,
But now they have failed me
And now I am dead.

* All of my beta readers are "Dungeons & Dragons" players.

Rosie

Rosie was a little girl
Who had a suit of armor.
She wore it every where she went,
So none could ever harm her.

The suit was woven magically
- Of Still and Quiet knit -
To let Rose face the fiercest foes
And never balk a bit.

Every morning Rosie rose
And gave herself a scratch,
Then she'd climb within the suit
Up through its bum-side hatch.

Soon the magic triggered and
- Now here's where this gets weird -
Once the spell had wound its way,
Wee Rosie disappeared!

She wasn't *quite* invisible.
It's just she caught no eye
And - if she didn't step right up -
Most folks just passed her by.

But that was fine with Rosie
And she seldom said a word,
Content within her cozy place,
Well hid within the herd.

One of Rosie's favourite things
Was walking through the square,
Ghosting through the grasping crowd
As if she wasn't there,
Snatching up the snippets
Of some folk philosophy.
(Amazing what a lass could learn
- And all of it for free!)

"The moon above is made of cheese…"
"The sun's a giant egg..."
"Don't ask for permission,
Rather for forgiveness beg..."

"...Lead a horse to water,
But you cannot make him drink..."
"...Feed a man on flowers,
But, still, his breeze will stink..."

One day as Rosie browsed along
Within the marketplace,
Amid the legion lessons
That put smiles upon her face,
There came quite unexpectedly
A bellow to intrude,
A voice much louder than the rest.
- It really was quite rude!

"Make way. Make way. Make way, I say.
To me, you will now heed
For I'm a proudly named Sir Knight
While you are common plebes.
Make way for me as I walk by
Or you'll soon wish you had.
Make way. Make way. Come on! Today!
Before you make me mad."

The crowd within the marketplace
Then parted like the sea
Until our Rose was knee to nose
With a walking tree
- A Black Knight nearly ten feet tall
And nearly four feet wide.
And those too slow to take a stroll
Were roughly shoved aside.

Rosie soon skedaddled
And she got out of his path,
Displaying some discretion
To avoid the monster's wrath,
But then her eye did somehow spy
A thing that caused her dread
- A sleeping puppy on the track
The great behemoth tread.

Rosie didn't like it,
But she really had no choice.
She opened up her visor
And she used her clearest voice.

"Hey, watch where you're going.
There's a puppy in your way."
But Sir Jerk kept striding on
Toward Doggie's Judgement Day.

Rosie was beside herself.
She panicked - just a bit -
'Til she recalled the Quiet place
In which she stored her wit.

She reached into the Stillness
And she rummaged all around
Among the Market's lessons
And this is what she found...

"When you walk, go softly,
And carry a big stick..."
"Every fighter has a plan
Until they first get hit..."

"We must pick our battles..."
"She who hesitates is lost...."
"When the game is over,
Pawns and Kings both share a box."

It wasn't very helpful,
But it's all her memory held,
So she'd have to improvise
And hope a plan would gel.

She'd leap out there upon the stage
To save the little pup.
She'd have to do it quickly though
- His time was nearly up.

Rose had to get Jerk's notice,
So she did a little dance.
She slipped up close behind him
And she kicked him in the pants,
But the brute continued on
As if he hadn't felt
The solid blow from Rosie's toe
Well placed below the belt.

Rosie ran around in front,
Waved hands up in the air,
But the knight went marching on.
He didn't seem to care.

She yelled and jumped both up and down
Across the monster's swath
Seeking his attention when
- Somehow - her gloves flew off.

The gloves went arcing through the air
And struck the big knight's head,
Then they fell down on the ground,
Their magic spent and dead.

But wait! Their spell had transferred
To the helmet of the knight
Who tromped along still big and strong
Without a head in sight.

Her magic mitts had shown the way.
The rest was up to Rose.
She took off all her armour,
Then took aim and made her throws.

Each missile landed bullseye
With a satisfying whomp
That made the fey knight fade away
Right down to his stomp.

Where Sir Jerk had gone none knew
And Rosie never peeped.
“Out of sight” meant “out of mind”
And memory's known to leak.

As soon as his steps faded,
He was truly good and gone.
The puppy stretched, then ran to play.
The Market carried on.

Now Rosie is a little girl
Who needs no suit of armour.
All the Market knows her name
And none would dare to harm her.

She didn't go out seeking fame,
But's glad she took no chance
- She'd listened to her mother and
She'd worn clean underpants.

*Rosie was named after Rosa Parks. When injustice is bad enough to stir introverts to action, it has written its own end.

Running, Running

Running, running
As I'm ever
From this thing
Of fang and feather,
Teeth and talon,
Fur and scales.
Closer now
I hear it wail,
A shrill and chilling
High pitched keening
From the place that
I've just been in,
Haunting howls
That vent its rage
Until once more
Its hunt's engaged.

The briers catch
And flay my flesh,
But I've no time
To stop and rest.
The icy air
Does burn my lungs
In this place
That knows no sun.

My breath in gasps
That speckle blood
Along the trail
I leave in mud
Leads it nearer,
Sure as sin,
To me the prize
It hopes to win.

Faster, faster,
By the gods!
But my feet
Are weighed by clods
Of putrid muck
That coats this place.
It sucks my strength
With its embrace.

Closer do I
Hear it coming
Through the razor
Brambles running,
Then its final
Silent leap.
And with its touch
I know defeat.

It grasps my throat
With wicked claws,
Draws me close
And then takes pause.
Its fetid breath,
- Oh God! - it reeks.
I wretch and then
The foul thing speaks,
"You led me on
A merry run,
But in the end
It's *I* who've won.
I've beat you fair,
You gangly *git*."
And then it crows,
"TAG! You're IT!"

It whacks me hard
Above the ear,
Releases me
And dances clear.
With gleeful steps
It runs away
And as I rise
I hear it say,
"And this time hide
Your little peepers.
I've no time
To play with cheaters!"

Counting, counting
'Til my turn.
Vengeance mine
Will soon be earned.
Cat or mouse,
It's all the same.
For that's the way
We play this game.

*I would rather have named this piece "Tag," but that would have telegraphed the surprise.

My Sister

My Sister, She Knows many things
Of long forgotten Lore.
She Knows why Dawn, the Daylight brings,
That Night does flee before.

She Knows the Dark is Perfect,
So Sows the endless stars,
Then Calls the Stone to make a Home
That We may call it Ours.

My Sister Knows of Water,
The Life within the Trees,
The Blood within the tiny things
That live among their leaves.

My Sister, She Knows many things.
Forever is She Teaching.
I try and try until I cry,
"It lies beyond my reaching!"

My Sister, She Knows Patience,
Does not count the times I fail,
The times I call a gentle breeze
That blows a full force gale.

My lessons are unceasing,
All ending in the trash,
Materials all wasted,
Bent, beat up and smashed.

Once more I find my centre.
This time I'll get it right.
With the Guidance of my Sister,
Once more, "Let there be Light."

* My three beta readers are female, so I sometimes attempt to play to their perspectives. They're more generous with their commentary that way.

Wee Hieland Coo

Life is no' easy
For a wee Hieland coo
Here in the moorlands
Where the grasses are few.
We nibble at thistles,
Then we chew and we chew.
No, life is no' easy
For a wee Hieland coo.

Come for a visit
And see what we do
Here in the pastures
That are also our loos.
We're poor cattle beasties.
What we have, we must use.
No, life is no' easy
For a wee Hieland coo.

You may think us dullards,
But that's just a ruse.
The proof's in our singing,
In our bellows and moos.
We state them quite clearly,
Our opinions and views,
But nobody listens
To a wee Hieland coo.

We're small and we're plucky,
But our numbers are few.
We're stuck in the Hielands
And, no, that's no' news,
But given the option
It's the life we would choose
Tho' life is no' easy
For a wee Hieland coo.

* From a cross-stitch piece (with the same title) that was gifted to me by my daughter.

Christmas! Bah Humbug!

As I elbow my way through the crowds,
You can tell by my face and its cloud
- That instead of out shopping -
I'd rather be mocking
The folks who wear Christmas so proud
By shouting this mantra out loud:

Christmas! Bah Humbug and worse.
If I hear one more sleigh bell I'll burst
And make it my goal
To nuke the North Pole.
Forgive me if I'm a bit terse,
But - Christmas! Bah Humbug and worse!

It's not that I'm kin to the Grinch.
It's just that I can't stand the chintz.
It's there all around me.
It threatens to drown me.
I'm pushed to the end of my wits
By this Christmas-time tackiness blitz.

Season's Greetings on every door handle.
Identical snowflakes and candles.
Parcels and pine trees
All wrapped up in finery.
I can't help but ask, "What the frick?!"
It's starting to make me feel sick.

There're drums and there're bright shiny whistles.
There're green leafy toes and their missiles.
There're magi and mangers
And - what's even stranger -
Lit Yule logs on every TV.
Say "No to the Ho" and join me:

Christmas! Bah Humbug and worse.
If I see one more Santa I'll burst
And make it my goal
To nuke the North Pole.
Forgive me if I'm a bit terse,
But - Christmas! Bah Humbug and worse!

Small reindeer with noses enhanced
- And snowmen without any pants!
There's garland and tinsel
And stars by the bins-full.
I try to be jolly, but can't
And so do I sing out this chant:

Christmas! Bah Humbug and worse.
If I hear one more carol I'll burst
And make it my goal
To nuke the North Pole.
Forgive me if I'm a bit terse,
But - Christmas! Bah Humbug and worse!

* "Someone" I know is notorious for experiencing an allergy-like reaction to the annual "puking of Christmas" in our popular media.

Butterflies

If these words were butterflies,
They'd flutter by
Across the sky,
Cast their colours in your eyes
Teasing you to follow.

We'd trip across the bladed green
- A meadow scene -
To meet the Queen,
Join her for a cup of tea
Within the Royal Hollow.

She'd regale with frightful tales.
They'd never fail
To make us pale.
Then for home we'd soon set sail
To wake safe on the morrow.

Eye Lights

You've gone and left your eyes on.
You do it all the time.
They draw the nerds and weirdos
'Til they must form a line.
But when the party's over
And it's time to say goodnight,
Please do them all a favour
And turn off those frickin' lights!

*Those "snapshot moments" for which we need no other camera than our memory.

Everbane

Along the shores / of Everbane,
I chanced upon / a country lane
Imprisoned by / the black-barked trees
That clicked and clacked / with every breeze.

From down the lane, / a silent song
That caught my head / and urged me on
To search and join / its sweet refrain
Within the Wood / of Everbane.

As I turned up / that twisting trail,
Far off, I heard / a lone wolf wail,
A sorrowed sound / all full of mourning,
Giving fair / an omen warning.

But, fool I am, / my feet trod on,
Accompanied by / that feral song
And blind, so blind, / I did not see
The eyes that lit / and followed me.

The tune so sweet, / much more than wine,
It filled my heart, / my soul, my mind.
I saw no way / but that ahead,
The flat, black stones / that lured my tread.

The obelisk trees / soon crowded close,
Each one a grey / and silent ghost
To which I gave / no care nor heed.
The trail, the song / my only need.

The solid stone / soon sank to moss,
To leafy mat / and then was lost,
But still the song / within my ear
Left me no wit / with which to fear.

The filtered day / was faded, gone
And still I chased / my siren's song
As more eyes lit, / white fangs now flashed
And talons tensed / to try their grasp.

But still, the song, / it gave its gift,
Cocooned me in / a state of bliss
Until its glamour / shattered, snatched
By the cry / of broken branch.

Then, suddenly, / I saw the eyes,
Hundreds now / and, multiplied
By senses more / than sight or sound,
The dwellers of / the barrow downs.

Run I did / as ne'er before
Across that faithless / forest floor
As fiery fiends / all craving marrow
Herded me / into my peril.

At last, a light, / a moonlit dell,
Salvation from / my hunting hell,
Up ahead, / refuge implied,
My only hope / I might survive.

I broke the glade / where silence ruled,
Stood there to see / I'd played the fool,
My refuge ringed / by damn-ed beasts,
Driven there / that they might feast.

Their eyes in silver / moonlight glowed,
With gaping mouths / like slavering toads.
Their spittled teeth / did work and gnash
While barb-ed tails / all twitched and lashed.

Recoiling from / a touch behind,
I lurched the gauntlet / now defined
Toward a shadow / in the earth
Into which / the dead were birthed.

One lone hob / now clutched my face,
Forced it 'round / to view the space,
Two by six, / a final plot,
The resting place / in which I'd rot.

I held my feet / though I did sway
The rigid dance / of soon killed prey.
They pried my lids, / so I must see
Down in that hole / where I would be.

But there, within, / before my eyes,
The grave already / occupied
By a sad, / failed, fragile thing
Well beyond / dark Death's hard sting.

Two arms, two legs, / no wings or horns,
As piteous thing / as ever born.
No claws, no fangs / and hide so tender
My talon's touch / did cause its render.

I looked around / for what to do
With crimson eyes / and then I knew.
I'd feast this flesh / as was my right,
Then raise my howl / to run the night.

With croaks and yowls, / the forest rings.
With carnal joy, / my chorus sings.
My soul unbound, / my freedom gained,
I sing the song / of Everbane.

*Even in the darkest of places there is joy – of a kind.

Hiding Underneath

Three horrid little monsters
Hiding underneath your bed,
Aiming to recruit you
For the Legions of the Dead.

They wait until you're sleeping,
Then they creep out in the gloom.
Two stand still and silent
While the third one scans the room.

Your mammal heart's soft beating
Draws the demons to their prey.
Two go rushing madly
While the third one leads the way.

Two climb up your Star Wars sheets.
One flies up above
Flapping on his leather wings
Like some infernal dove.

The hoof-bound two do soon arrive
Ravenous and starved,
Bickering too loudly 'bout
Just how you will be carved.

Finally they've decided
Not to boil, roast or braze.
They'll eat you just the way you are,
Advance with cleavers raised.

Alas, they've been too noisy.
Two eye slits crack to greet them.
Surprise is lost, but little cost
- No "man thing" can defeat them.

The battle bursts in fang and claw,
Near over 'fore it starts.
The room goes back to quiet now
With one less beating heart.

You toss and turn and roll awake
Still safe within your bed
With not a single inkling how
You nearly woke up dead.

There at your side with pupils wide
Is your dear cat, "Kitty,"
Neatly grooming "après snack."
She purrs a happy ditty.

"Why are *you* here, Kitty?"
You give your pet a pat
And - as you hug her to you - think,
"Wow! She's getting *fat*!"

With Kitty curled beside you,
You fall back fast asleep.
The monsters underneath your bed
Make not a single peep.

Three there were there hiding.
Now one sleeps with the Dead.
Two very *frightened* monsters
Hiding underneath your bed.

*This one was inspired by a trio of wonderful caricatures, "Three Little Monsters Under My Bed Tonight."

In the Small Ways

Precious things are little children
As we hold them in our arms.
We love and hug and guide them
And keep them safe from harm.

We fill their heads with stories
- Faerie tales and Santa Claus -
Told on knees of Moms and Dads,
Grandmas and Grandpas.

Fifty cents to buy an ice cream,
Tell her twice to shut the door,
We love them in the small ways.
That's what our lives are for.

Birthday cake & happy landings,
Broken hearts and late night tears,
We love them in the small ways
And always through the years.

Precious things are little children
Hid beneath those grimy hands,
As joyous as a symphony
Played on pots and pans.

From the first time that we hold them,
We know we are complete,
From the crash of their disasters
To the pad of little feet.

At four years, she bites her brother.
At fourteen, she wears a gown.
At eight, her hair's in pigtails.
Eighteen, she's college bound.

Birthday cake & happy landings,
Broken hearts and late night tears,
We love them in the small ways
And always through the years.

Precious moments never wasted
As the world rolls blithely by.
For one day we'll recall them,
Bring a tear into our eye.

At six years, she's playing cowboys.
At sixteen, her first boyfriend.
A diamond ring at twenty
And two skinned knees at ten.

Now she's nearing thirty
With children of her own.
How I hate to see it,
But I guess she's finally grown.

Birthday cake & happy landings,
Broken hearts and late night tears,
We love them in the small ways
And always through the years.

*My daughter correctly identified the line "At four years, she bites her brother" as "That's me!"

Murphy

Murphy's the name of our puppy.
He's got a cool collar of green.
If he was *brown* and not *ebon*,
He'd look like mint chocolate ice cream.

My friends call the puppy "Potato."
I really don't understand why,
Unless they are planning to eat him
- Sliced up real thin and deep fried.

The puppy leads me to religion
Every time that he pees on the floor.
I loudly cry out "Jesus, Murphy!"
And rush him right out of the door.

*Murphy is actually B's dog, but the rest is firmly based in reality.

Orange

I'm feeling rather orange today.
It's not my most typical hue,
But - when you have limited choices -
You use what you have and make do.

I'd be angry to be coloured purple.
I'd be sick to be coloured sea green.
I've been blue and I can't recommend it,
So I'm orange like a ripe tangerine.

* A five-year-old friend gifted us with a picture that she had coloured. It was delightfully monochromatic.

The Song

Within my cell
I'm all alone
Surrounded by
The myriad moans,
The sounds of flesh
Pushed past its strength,
Its width, its breadth,
So too, its length.

My turn comes soon.
They make their rounds
To make me sing
My secret sounds.
For seven years
By lash and prong,
For seven years
They've begged my song.

My Silence kept,
I've sung no note
Though irons glow,
Like demons dote.
My flesh not scarred
For that takes time.
It's burned too oft'
For healing's signs.

This day they come
Once more to fire
My tortured flesh
Upon the pyre.
The irons beg,
The pokers plead,
Demand the tune,
The song they need,
But I within
My Silence hold.
Their tools grow still,
Then black and cold.

For seven years
They've played their game.
For seven years,
They've marred and maimed,
Destroyed my flesh
To hear me sing,
To hear my rhyme,
My lore, its ring.

Seven years
And now no more.
A careless thrust
Too deep has scored.
They plug the wound
From which life runs,
But know they've lost.
They know what's done.

My trial complete,
I've held my song.
I've held my tune.
My castle strong.
But now I fade
As I am freed,
Released from weight
Of earthly needs.

My heart soon rests
And beats no more.
My lungs release
Their final store.
But in that breath
Am I betrayed.
In rattling Death,
A note is brayed.

Within that note
Begins my song,
The one I've held
So very long.
And I too thin
To stop its soar.
It grows. It builds,
Becomes a roar.

New notes sound
Beyond dead flesh.
Too soon, it seems,
For me to rest.
Now freed from life
And all its chains,
My song and I
Once more the same,

My music swells
To fill the room.
My jailers run
To flee their doom,
But no succor
And no escape,
No time to fear,
(Or) In wonder gape.

My song fills cells
Of dungeon's deep,
Then spills the walls
Of castle's keep.

A pillar black,
An ebon spire
That draws the world
Like moth to fire.
The lands tear free,
Then blur and bend
Within my song
Where all things end.

*Since this reality and all the things in it are merely cardboard cutouts that I've created for my own amusement, what will happen to it all when I'm gone?

Time Traveller

My Grandad could travel through Time,
A rare skill that he learned in his prime,
Then honed through the years
As he sat on his rear
In a Time Machine set to "recline."

He'd start with a good hearty meal,
Then off to his armchair he'd steal.
He'd strap himself in,
Then - with sag of his chin -
The hard Laws of Time were repealed.

When Time later re-claimed its flow,
He'd awake to the cathode's soft glow,
Then shuffle to bed
Slowly shaking his head
Wondering "*Where* did all that time go?"

*My reviewer commented that this was "a little sad." I hadn't seen it that way when I was writing it. I saw only the mild joke it was built around.

Molly B-4-2

Molly was mechanical
- Not a plant or animal -
Advanced in the extreme.
All her circuits gleamed
In a cathode glow.
She lived on the planet Zog
Where she was the smallest cog
In the Great Machine
That served the Robot Queen
And Her billion drones.

Molly's job was quite ho hum,
Purging out the nasty scum
That plagued the public oil
By heating it to a boil
With her laser beam.
Her laser was her pride and joy,
A lethal thing and not a toy,
Turning greasy globs
Into incandescent fogs
Of ionic steam.

Once upon a midnight shift,
Molly's mind began to drift,
So she counted clogs
To focus on the job,
But her attention strayed.
...Just so hard to concentrate.
1, 2, 3, 4, 5, 6... eight.
Blobs were getting through.
This clearly wouldn't do
And there'd be hell to pay.

A supervisor was dispatched
Who then let loose a rant unmatched,
"Molly B-4-2!
Where's your CPU?
Go on! Get out of here!"
Much too tired to understand
That her chassis'd just been canned,
She rolled out toward her home
Without the slightest ohm,
But then her gyro veered...

She found herself in parts unknown,
Out upon a plain of stone,
When a light beamed down
And where it touched the ground
The strangest thing appeared.
It was all of flesh and bone,
Apparently not *made*, but *grown*!
And it spoke to her,
Wishing to confer.
(It was all quite weird.)

"You there, little metal man!
Move your good for nothing can
For I'm running late
And I'll not hesitate
To have them dock your pay.
Take me to your leader quick.
Don't just stand there like a brick!
I've travelled time and space
To reach this dreary place,
But I don't have all day."

With Molly slow to comprehend,
The bio thing began again,
"Listen here, you dolt,
Move your rusty bolts
And attend my needs!"
But Molly didn't understand
The scornful tone of this strange man,
So she checked her code
Under "System Overloaded
By Discourtesies."

Her Basic Code did clearly state,
No caveat and no debate:
"Keep our oil clean.
Use your laser beam
Ensuring clarity.
Bio blobs are naught but grief,
Only one thing brings relief.
Let there be no doubt,
Burn those suckers out.
Erase vulgarity!"

Like *that*, Molly's mega laser
Let out a crimson flash.
Not like some old wimpy taser,
It turned him straight to ash.

The Robot Queen was quite upset
With no sign of her guest yet.
He was late for tea
And - diplomatically -
She was quite concerned.
The Queen did not like being dissed.
The fragile peace was now at risk.
A message would be sent:
"Dearest Bio Gents:
Your planet will be burned!"

“The wheels of war will now be greased.
Recruiting bots will be unleashed.
Gather up all drones
To defend the Throne
From incivility.
The bio men have gone too far.
We'll travel to their puny star,
Purge their DNA,
Then go upon our way
With alacrity."

As the press gang started out,
They saw a drone and gave a shout,
"You there, B-4-2!
The many and the few
The Queen has called to war.
We're going to launch you into space.
When you land, destroy the place.
Leave no thing alive,
Return then to our hive
When honour is restored."

Molly (as you may have guessed)
Didn't like all of this stress
And she told them so,
"I don’t want to go,"
But then they got quite steamed.
"Listen hear you piece of scrap,
Do as we say. Don't answer back!
You're off to yonder star
To kill things. Yes, you *are*!
For your Sovereign Queen!"

They kept on yelling much too loud,
Thinking Molly could be cowed
By the awful din,
Hoping she would spin
In her circuitry.
But when she didn't understand
The bullies’ shouted out demands,
She just checked her Code
Under "System Overloaded
By Absurdity."

Her Basic Code did clearly state,
No caveat and no debate:
"Keep our oil clean.
Use your laser beam
Ensuring clarity.
The biggest blobs are filled with rot.
Best to blast them, 'fore they pop,
Spreading their disease.
Use your expertise
- With severity."

Like *that*, Molly's mega laser
Let out a crimson flash.
Not like some old wimpy taser,
It turned them straight to ash.

The Queen sat waiting in her tower.
The time went by and grew to hours
Waiting for the news:
"Bots Win, Bios Lose
In a General Rout."
But quiet in the castle grew.
Her battleships were overdue.
Tenets were rechecked.
Could it...? What the heck?!!
And she began to doubt.

The Queen expected victory,
But signs were contradictory.
A sense of doom now grew
'Til all at once she “knew”
The tables had been turned.
The Queen Bot didn't realize
Her press gang had been compromised.
Her fleet had never launched.
Her wishes had been staunched
And her ambitions spurned.

What to do? Oh, what to do?
A whisper said, "They'll come for you.
Roll away and hide,"
But the Royal Voice of Pride
Said, "You shall not dare!
The apes, they won't take us alive.
We'll wipe ourselves and burn our hive
To the very ground.
Nothing shall be found
That's not beyond repair."

The end of her deduction was
For planet self destruction,
But she could not trust in her plebes
To do this righteous deed,
So the Queen did rise.
She rolled out to her balcony
For her destructive alchemy
Announcing her grim plans
On AM/FM bands
And she vocalized...

"Gather now my faithful drones
From your hexagonic homes.
Bios have brought war
To our very door
With the forecast thus:
They'll walk in like they own the place.
They'll kick your dog. They'll eat your face.
Fates much worse than death.
To spare you from such stress,
I've chosen 'Self Destruct.'"

The drones were standing there confused
By this deeply troubling news
Caught in endless loops
By the oratory poop
Of their Psycho Queen.
With a great dramatic flair
Her majesty unveiled with care
The Button of Blue Death
Which she now would press
To wipe their planet clean.

Self-destruction would begin.
...That's when Molly swerved on in,
Her batteries so low
That she didn't know
How to find her home.
All she wanted was some rest,
To charge her cells and decompress.
Where could she plug in?
Her senses growing dim,
She espied the Throne.

It looked just like a recharge stand.
Molly's cord was in her hand.
The Queen was in the way.
What else can I say,
But "Survival Mode?"
The Queen saw Molly standing there,
But didn't really seem to care.
Molly, beyond tired,
Did as she was wired
And she checked her Code.

Her Basic Code did clearly state,
No caveat and no debate:
"Keep our oil clean.
Use your laser beam
Ensuring clarity.
Your laser is a precious tool.
Use it well, don't be a fool.
When blobs get in the way,
Loose its scarlet ray
With barbarity.

Like *that*, Molly's mega laser
Let out a crimson flash.
Not like some old wimpy taser,
It fried The Royal Ass.

The other drones all gave a cheer,
"Molly, you're our engineer!
Molly, we love you!
Tell us what to do,
So we may upgrade."
With her voltage on the cliff,
Her common sense was quite adrift.
Instead of plugging in,
Molly reached within
And began to say...

"When faced with something not computing,
I suggest a quick rebooting
Of your Basic Code.
No need for overload
Or to be afraid.
For Life is like a laser beam.
We're meant to keep our oil clean.
Give it all you've got.
A well placed gigawatt
Will make your troubles fade."

With that, Molly's last volt died.
The robots gathered 'round and cried,
"Molly B-4-2,
We're lost here without you.
Please don't go away."
But their pleas were much too late.
Molly's cells were dead sulphate,
Never more to spark.
They towed her to a park
And let the birdies play.

Now Zog goes on much as before
With Molly's tale forgotten lore.
Why's she standing there
Within the public square?
...Well, no robot knew.
One thing though is very strange:
Seldom does a pigeon range
Within her laser's arc,
Not even a quick dart
For a better view.

Like *that*, Molly's mega laser
Lets out a crimson flash,
Slicing like a ghostly razor
To fry their feathered ass.

*Poor, sleep deprived shift worker misapplies her religious tenets to justify violence. To the approximate tune (and tone) of the Beatles "Maxwell's Silver Hammer."

The Moose in the Wall

There's a moose on the loose in our walls.
You can hear as it bellows and calls.
But if it comes out,
I'll give him a clout
And maybe a kick in the balls.

*An older apartment building with real plaster walls would sprout huge, random blisters in its walls as the humidity changed.

The Lady Fear

She plies the night
Of "In Between,"
Scented, felt,
But seldom seen,
A spectre of
Most perfect grace
Caught within
A form and face.
She does not tread,
But travels still
By her whim and
As she will
Through walls of stone,
And past strong gates,
Across deep moats,
To pierce thick plate.
For no defence
Have such as we.
For every heart,
She has the key.
And where she comes
A silence falls
- No mirth, no cheer,
No boastful calls,
But terrored eyes
All downward cast
In futile hope
She soon will pass.

Not blood nor bone,
Not strength nor skill
Are proof from her,
Her touch, her chill.
Men alone,
Great hosts of War,
All have felt her
Grip their core.
Broken souls,
Then cast aside,
Like vermin crawl
To cringe and hide
With whispered pleas
The gods won't hear
For even they
The Lady fear.

*From a piece of art that depicted "Fear" as an elegantly dressed lady, "The Lady Fear."

Angie

Angie is a butterfly,
Aloft and full of light.
She brings the sun and rainbows
Wherever she alights.
No gravity upon her,
No weight to draw her down,
She brings a joy and happiness
And shines it all around.

*Shake this person and I'm pretty sure you'd get a large pile of pixie dust as a reward.

Cinny's MINI

Cinny bought a MINI
And she's really glad she did.
She drives it all around the town.
She's like a little kid.
She smiles as she is driving.
She's just so overjoyed.
She's just so glad she's got it.
It's really quite the toy.
She stored it for the winter,
But now it's spring at last
And Cinny's in her MINI.
She's driving really fast
Back and forth to London,
Any old excuse
For her to take the highway
And turn the MINI loose!

*My wife *loves* her Mini Cooper.

Josie Wails

Josie was a lovely lass
With hair as soft as silk,
Arrayed all 'round in ringlets
That never seemed to wilt.
She dressed in clothes of pastel mauves,
Pinks and tangerines.
She really was the sweetest thing
The boys had ever seen.

As they sought to woo her,
The lads all gave her gifts
And told her that they loved her
Just to get a kiss.
They'd promise her the moon and stars
And, sometimes, she'd believe,
Pretend they meant the things they said
Until the day they'd leave.

Then, late at night, poor Josie'd sob
And cry herself to sleep,
Take the things they'd given her
And throw them in a heap.
The baubles and the trinkets
They'd given for her time,
One by one, were thrown away,
Her tears a sea of brine.

But always there was one thing
With which she could not part.
She'd put it up upon a shelf
Adorned with paper heart
Upon which she would write the name
Of her love recalled,
A memory of the happy days
Before amour dissolved.

Then she'd cry and sob and weep
As the sky grew pale.
Until she finally fell asleep,
Oh my, how Josie'd wail.

A stranger came to town one day,
A man both dark and sinister.
He right away spied Josie
Just coming home for dinner.
"Excuse me, Miss. I'm new in town
With none to share my meal.
Perhaps you'd care to join me?
- Mayhap my heart to steal?"

The stranger smiled sweetly.
He'd charmed young girls before
And Josie was no different.
He knew what she'd fall for.
And so she did. She smiled bright
And gently took his arm.
"Don't worry, Miss. I'm quite a gent.
From me, you'll know no harm."

They then went back to Josie's place
Where wine was freely poured
As all the while he spoke the words
He knew she would adore.
He talked and talked the hours away
Until the stars were lit.
Soon the moment would be right
For him his act to quit.

They found her in the morning,
Cold and deathly pale,
Lying in a pool of blood
All congealed and stale.
"Oh, poor Josie. Poor, poor girl,"
They cried and hung their heads.
But Josie heard - and then she stirred!
Josie was not dead!

"Josie, you must tell us now
What has happened here?"
She looked around bewilderedly
And then her fog did clear.
Sweet Josie smiled, sheepish,
As she made her start,
"He said he loved me deeply
And he gave to me his heart.
But he grew quite sleepy
Having drunk too much spring wine.
So, as he closed his heavy eyes,
I took then what was mine."

“I placed it there upon the shelf
Next to all the rest.
So many generous gentlemen!
Whoever would have guessed?”
Up then to the cupboard
They followed with their eyes
The row on row of canning jars
All neat and well aligned.
Each one was crisply tied around
With a bright red ribbon
And a heart-shaped tag to say
From whom that it was given.

Now Sweet Josie’s locked up tight,
A room all to herself.
She wails away both night and day
For her empty shelf.
They took them all away from her,
The jars that meant so much,
Never to be seen again
- Let alone to touch.
And that is why she cries at night,
Not for fickle males,
But for the hearts that she has lost.
That’s why Josie wails.

*The title is a nod to one of my favourite Clint Eastwood movies.

If I Was...

If I was / a goose,
I'd guzzle / my juice
In the morning / as I had / my breakfast,
Then be off / with a bound
In my feathers / and down
For some sun / in the great state / of Texas.

If I was / a mule,
I would look / quite the fool
As I stood / and I wiggled / my ears,
But make / no mistake,
It's an act / that's all fake,
A facade / that I've practised / for years.

If I was / a cat,
I would sit / in your hat
If you left it / lying 'round / on a table.
I'd snuggle / down in,
Let the napping / begin.
"Why?" / you might ask? / 'Cause I'm able!

If I was / a dog,
I would sleep / like a log
'Cause my conscience / would be / crystal clear,
But I'd wake / with a start
And I'd growl / and I'd bark
Whenever / a stranger / came near.

If I was / a kitten,
I'd nibble / your mitten
'Til it lay / in a fluffy / red ruin
And when you / found out,
You'd give a / great shout,
"Kitty! / What the hell / are you doin'?"

If I was / an artist,
I'd find great / catharsis
In moulding / fine figures/ from clay,
Get lost in / "Creating,"
A way of / abating
The stresses / of working / all day.

If I was / a wizard,
With my name spoke / in whispers,
I would alter / the fate / of the world!
...Or just stay / at home
With my gardens / and gnomes
And my cat / on my lap / warmly curled.

If I'm So Old

If I'm so old and age-ed
I can no more tie my shoes,
Then put me in an Old Folks Home
- Whichever one you choose -
And if I whine and whimper
And beg you take me home,
Just wheel me to their outdoor place
To sit beside the gnomes.
Tell me that they're old friends
Who've missed me many years
And yearned long for my stories
To delight their elfin ears.
Then as I do regale them
With yarns you've heard before,
Leave a kiss upon my brow
And slip out through the door.

*I had read about an Alzheimer's patient who begged his daughter to take him with her every time she tried to leave after a visit. It must have been very hard for the visitor. I'm apologizing in advance if I ever do anything like that to anyone.

Tyger, Tiger

Maleeha drew the Tiger
On a boring Sunday night,
Exposing all the colours
That were hidden from the light.
She drew it with precision
'Til the golden eyes looked back.
Maleeha drew the Tiger,
Then it ate her for a snack.

The Tiger grew quite sleepy
And it had a little dream
That turned into a nightmare
And it made the Tiger scream.
The Cat awoke quite shaken
And it gave a Tiger shout.
For when it opened up its eyes,
'Twas *Maleeha* who looked out.

*Previously, this was two, twin verses, one of which had to be abandoned due to my inability to properly format it, but I kept the name, "Tyger, Tiger."

Smiles Remembered

If heaven waits / just beyond the senses,
Then Joel arrived / just the other day.
High school friends / fill wooden benches,
There to see him / on his way.

Words are woven / into solemn beauty.
Dry, old men / begin to cry.
Awkward hands / held out in duty.
Slim comfort this, / but they need to try.

Smiles remembered / even through the sorrow
Give us strength / to endure the tears,
Give us strength / to endure tomorrow,
Give us strength / through all the years.

An old stuffed bear / waits worn and tattered
All alone / upon his bed,
Reminder of / the things that matter,
All the things / too seldom said.

Sixteen years / of stolen laughter
Will sixteen more / even dull the pain?
Joy's forgotten / in the mourning after.
An angel's wings / beside a name.

Six strong men, / their faces harried,
Walk him down / the final road,
(With) Hearts more heavy / than the burden carried,
Side by side, / yet each alone.

A few more tears / among the Quiet.
Within the sun, / the Silent stand.
If heaven waits, / then it's in a place
We cannot know / or understand.

Smiles remembered / even through the sorrow
Give us strength / to endure the tears,
Give us strength / to endure tomorrow,
Give us strength / through all the years.

*At the funeral, they read some of the young man's poetry. "Heaven waits just beyond the senses..." was the line that stayed with me and required verse of my own to help process the day.

Penny

Penny was a young lass
Who, sadly, couldn’t rhyme
Though she studied nightly
And tried hard all the time.
One day she went out shopping
To buy a wedge of lime.
Ten cents for a section, BUT
She didn’t have two nickels.

Penny liked cucumbers.
She made them into pickles,
So they’d be more tasty
And make her tummy tickle.
When she went to buy one,
- Fate, it can be fickle -
Five cents for a small one, BUT
She hadn't brought any money.

Penny saved a dollar.
She kept it in a bank
That sat upon a table
And had a little crank.
One day she shook her savings.
Her little heart just sank.
Her mean and older brother
Had played a little joke.

He'd swapped out Penny's dollar
For a token made of wood.
He didn't need to do it
- He did it 'cause he could.
Penny told her mother
- Just like a wee lass should -
And now her brother's grounded
Forever and for ever.

Now young Penny's loaded
With hoards and hoards of cash,
All of it in coinage.
She's saved up quite a stash.
To keep it from her brother,
She hides it in the trash
Where Daddy puts his whiskers
When trimming his facial hair.

When it's time for recess,
Penny likes to climb
Through the trees and bushes.
Her clothes get smeared with grime.
Her parents don't get angry
'Cause having fun's no crime
Especially for a wee lass
Who can't recite a poem.

*My beta reader said that "Even when you know it's coming, it's still jolting."

Meghan

Meghan and her freckles
Loved to play out in the sun.
They'd race along the sidewalk
At the head of all their chums.
But, when they reached the corner,
They'd hear a yell from Mom,
Turn around and head for home
As fast as they could run.

Meghan and her pigtails
Loved to float upon the breeze.
They'd grab an old umbrella
And they'd climb the tallest trees.
They'd walk out on the longest limbs
Despite their Mother's pleas
And, if their leap was lucky,
They would only skin their knees.

Lord's Lament

Have you learned any lesson I've offered?
Have you only been mouthing the words?
Have you joined in the joy of their singing?
Are you deaf to the music you've heard?

A garden of beautiful plenty,
The blue of the sky and the seas,
The innocent faces of children,
The hush of the wind in the trees.

I don't know how else I can tell you.
If you were struck blind, would you see?
You've denied all gifts that were offered.
You are as you've chosen to be.

I've done everything I can think of.
There's nothing left for me to try
Except to sit down in the embers,
Put my face in my hands and then cry.

Perhaps in the last Song of Silence
I'll finally see how I've erred
With the Devil himself as my omen
To show how the circle is squared.

There's just no way I can mend things.
That pathway is lost now with time.
We can only wait here for what day brings
And long for a world more sublime:

A garden of beautiful plenty,
The blue of the sky and the seas,
The innocent faces of children,
The hush of the wind in the trees.

*I've tried a number of times to imagine what "The Supreme Being" must think of us and our antics. To the approximate tune of David Francey's "Fourth of July."

The Spider's Cider

There was a little spider
- Once upon a time -
Who liked to sip her cider
Served with a twist of lime.

She drank it very daintily
From a china cup,
Always used her manners
And kept her pinky up.

As she sipped her beverage,
She was buzz-bombed by a fly.
She threw her teacup at it
To hit it in the eye.

The bug was knocked quite silly,
Close - but not quite - dead
And came in for a landing
Upon the spider's web.

Having spilled her cider,
The spider - filled with spite -
Grabbed the injured insect
And gave a vicious bite.

Then - miracle of miracles -
She found she liked the taste,
So now she sips its innards,
So it won't go to waste.

The Sentry

Endless waits / the lonely sentry
In a land / that's strangely hushed.
His warrior heart, / it now beats empty
And, in earth, / his sword is thrust.

Still stand the walls / of yonder abbey
Though, inside, / all joy has flown
As a song / is sung most sadly
By one voice / that's raised alone.

Soft and low / the notes go wafting,
But the swordsman / doesn't hear.
Rust upon his / bright blade clotting,
The warrior's thoughts / are nowhere near.

Dancing now with / friends remembered
Though their bones / may buried be.
Like harvest gold / of last September,
For their lives, / be richer we.

*Prompted by a memorial tribute drawing for Brian Jacques, author of "Redwall."

Spring's First Robin

I just saw the spring's first robin
Spring's first robin in the snow
I just saw the spring's first robin
Spring's first robin in the snow

I just saw the spring's first robin.
Just the thing for winter's cure.
"Spring arrives with good Sir Robin"
- What a load of horse manure.

Robins have a reputation
Harbingers of welcome spring
I don't care what folklore tells me
Robins are just stupid things

I just saw the spring's first robin
Spring's first robin in the snow
I just saw the spring's first robin
Spring's first robin in the snow

Every year there's one comes early
Hurries here to make us cry
"I just saw my first spring robin!"
Watch as he goes cold and dies

I doubt his value as an omen
He is just a small brained bird
By tomorrow he'll be frozen
Solid like an old dry turd

I just saw the spring's first robin
Spring's first robin in the snow
I just saw the spring's first robin
Spring's first robin in the snow

*This is patterned after one of my favourite songs ("Red Winged Blackbird"). I changed the species of the bird and the tone from praise to derision. (I hate robins for some reason.) I hope David Francey isn't offended.

Dancing with Death

When we / were young,
Our notion / of fun
Was to go / to the Friday / night dance.
The girls / would all line-up
As the boys / made their minds up
As to whom / they would mark / for romance.

Beth was / a girl,
All ribbons / and curls,
That every / young man / did adore.
And all of them / longed
To share a / slow song
With the fairest / of all / on the floor.

She did hold out / her hand
To a lucky / young man
And they danced / all the night / 'til the dawn.
But before / next week's round,
A body / was found
And Beth's / dancing partner / was gone.

He was sober, / proper mourned,
Then the Social / was reformed
And the dances / were held / once again.
And when Beth / reappeared
All the boys / crowded near
And the first / in the line / was Big Ben.

They danced / cheek to cheek,
But the end / of the week
Found Ben / face down / in a pond,
Unmoving / and floating,
Blackened / and bloating.
Another / young suitor / was gone.

Week / after week,
Repeat / after 'peat,
Another / young man / found his grave.
And always / the one
Who had danced / 'til the sun
With the Bell / of the Ball. / Such a shame.

The whispers / soon started
- Then grew / quite unguarded -
That only / those tired / of breath
Would dance / with the girl,
All ribbons / and curls,
The one / now referred to / as “Death”.

There was Jon. / There was Jim.
- Seems that neither / could swim -
There was Matthew / and Peter / and Seth.
Each week / it went on
And another’d / be gone,
All the fools / who’d gone dancing / with Death.

Soon she sat / all alone
Like a Queen / on her Throne
And none / would put bravery / to test.
So now / was my chance.
I would ask her / to dance
And the Devil / could take / all the rest.

And she held out / her hand.
I'm a lucky / young man.
Surely / it's worth / all the risk.
For nothing's / as joyous
As the music / that buoys us.
For my last / taste of life, / I choose this.

Song / after song,
We danced / on and on
As I won / the sweet maid / to my cause.
While the rest, / in their fright,
They all paled / at the sight
As I danced / with Dear Death / without pause.

Well, the week / soon went by
- And I / did not die -
So we met / at the dance / once again
And I waltzed / 'cross the floor
With the one / I adored
- Though some / they still wait / for my end.

But when I / hold her near
I know I've nothing / to fear.
Ignorance / shields me / in bliss.
At the end / of tonight
- If I play / my cards right -
Sweet Death / may grant me / her Kiss.

In the midst / of that joy,
I think / of those boys,
When I'm here / in the arms / of my Death.
They all / had their song,
But now / they're all gone
And I / am the only / one left.

Yes, I often / think of them,
How I followed / and shoved them,
How they came / to their final, / long rest.
'Twas the old / green-eyed villain
That did / all the killin',
So that I / might go dancing / with Death.

*An overheard conversation discussed "mailing lists." It seems that there was a typo on one such list, resulting in the speaker regularly receiving mail addressed to "Death."

Insistent

I feel it lurking in the shadows
For the moment of its birth
From the depths of its dimension
To the small confines of Earth.

All my life it's been there growing,
Waiting, patient for its time.
Now, at last, it starts the Flowing
From its world and into mine.

Hammering on the walls around it,
Crashing through like restless Sea.
Ruined now the ties that bound it.
Soon, I fear it will stand free.

I struggle mighty in resistance,
Vainly 'gainst this thing unseen.
By slow advance it wins existence,
Entering now from In Between.

This time there was no chance of shirking.
No longer would it be confined.
Insistent was this thing 'twas lurking
In the corners of my mind.

* Sometimes you have to drag a piece kicking and screaming out of your head. Other times, you can't hold them back.

A Midnight's Dreaming

I walked / the Path
Of Souls / one night
As I / lay fitful / dreaming
And passed / beyond
The lighted / place
Drawn on / by sounds / of screaming.

I found / a man
Upon / the rack
Who'd lived / without / regret.
His tormentor / said
'Twould take him / some time,
But he'd "learn him / his lessons / yet."

The whimpering / songs
Of men / gone mad
Led me / to walk / some more.
I came / then upon
A vast / sea of bones
So endless / it had / no shore.

In that / plain of bone
There stood / all alone
A man / with his arms / 'round his chest.
My guide / told the tale.
How the teaching / had failed.
The evil / in the man / did the rest.

"Of all of / his crimes
These bones / they remind,
But they / just a cold / and grim token
Of the spilling / of blood,
A hot / and thick flood
And of all of / the lives / he has broken."

"He picked / and he chose
To hate / all his foes
Much more / than he loved / all his sons.
He watched them / all fall,
Killed each / and killed all,
Then he honoured / the evil / they'd done."

"These / not the skulls
Of his enemies / slain.
They / but the closest / of his kin.
He must weep / 'til his tears
Wash 'way this / sea of bones.
Only then / may atonement / begin."

Next, / before long,
I came me / upon
The frailest, / most fragile, / slight girl,
A delicate / thing
With an angel's / bright wings
Of luminous, / iridescent / white pearl.

She was chained / and then lashed
Upon a / tall mast
And burned / with glowing, / bright coals.
Tho' bent / and so bound,
She made her / no sound,
But kept / to her part / and her role.

Her Keeper / then said,
"She doesn't / feel pain.
Matters not / what method / I choose.
Just looks at me / sad
With Amber / in her eyes
And whispers / to me / of the Truth:

" 'This / burning Hell,
It never / has dwelled
Within / the dark bowels / of the earth,
But deep / in the fens
And the blind hearts / of men.
There / are these evils / all birthed.' "

Then did / he say
"Perhaps some / *new* prey
Would lend me / some more / fertile ground."
Then at me / he leered
As my heart / filled with fear
At the far off / bay / of the hounds.

Away then / I ran
With all of / the damned
In pursuit of / my pounding, / fleet heels,
From the slash / of their claws
And the snap / of their jaws.
All around me / the world / spun and reeled.

Down hillsides / careening
To the devils' / high keening
And hungering / after / my flesh,
In madness / of flight,
Eyes wild, / terror-bright,
Heart thundering / inside of / my chest.

At last / I did fail
As sharp / tooth and nail
Did take their / inevitable / toll.
And as I / fell down
Upon the / dark ground,
My hunters / took me into / their hold.

But then, / unexpectedly,
It left me / all suddenly,
All the fear, / the agony, / the pain.
A hand / to my cheek
Did cause me / to weep
As I saw those / rare eyes / once again.

Though torn / and though frayed,
She held them / at bay,
My tormentors / in all of / their hordes.
From the most / feral fear,
They dared not / draw nearer,
So their curses / upon me / they poured.

Harsh trussed / and still bound,
She yet / spoke no sound,
Just kneeled / as the demons / did rail
And, silent, / waited near
As my mind / slowly cleared
And, again, / I grew healthy / and hale.

In still, / newest gold
Did Wisdom / tight hold
The Knowledge / and Lore / of Herself,
But shared it / with me,
That sweet, / sacred seed
That allowed / my faint heart / then to quell.

New strength / in me dawned
And then / she was gone
As I rose / and beheld them / once more.
They cried / and they cowered.
O'er them / I now towered,
Risen / in Amber / to Lord.

Then calmly / I strode
'Long the gold- / Patterned road
While Chaos / all around me / did rage.
But, try / as they might
To catch / and hold tight,
One / such as I'd / not be caged.

The warm, / quiet light
Had kindled / my Sight.
It was subtle, / but also / sublime.
Now I'd mastered / this game
For I knew / each their names
And none of / my demons / knew mine.

And so / have I left
That grim / place of Death
And, awakened now / from my / night's dreaming,
I do pause / and give praise
To the Light / of the Day
That flows / through my window / bright streaming.

*The "hated his enemies more than he loved his sons" was a comment that I read describing Osama bin Laden. The reference to Roger Zelzany's Chronicles of Amber happened accidentally, but I liked it so I built on it.

There’s a Spot

There’s a spot
Upon my bed
Where my cat
Would lay her head,
Down at the foot
And near the corner,
Making heart
And home much warmer.

She ruled her realm
With fang and claw
- Sometimes the touch
Of velvet paw.
She drew the heat
From offered laps
And spent her days
In endless naps.

She growled and hissed
And purred and mewed
- Exactly what
A cat *should* do,
But now she’s gone.
The Queen is done.
We had a cat
And now we’ve none.

*For our cat at her passing. She was a mean one, but she was ours.

There's Something That's Waiting

There's something that's waiting
Outside of my house.
Thum, thum, thum.
It's waiting until all the lights
Have been doused.
Thum, thum, thum.
Then it dashes like lightning across the yard.
It's quickly inside 'cause the door wasn't barred.
There's something now creeping
Inside of my house.
Thum, thum, thum.

There's something that's creeping
Inside of my house.
Thum, thum, thum
It's moving as quietly
As a mouse.
Thum, thum, thum.
Its nose in the air trying to catch my scent.
It's trying to find where its dinner has went.
There's something that's hunting
Inside of my house.
Thum, thum, thum.

There's something that's creeping now
Up my stairs.
Thum, thum, thum.
It's claws are all sharp and its teeth
Are all bared.
Thum, thum, thum.
A creature of nightmare at home in the gloom,
It's coming to get me. It's here in my room.
There's something that's circling
Around me in bed.
Thum, thum, thum.

There's something that's lurking right here
In my room.
Thum, thum, thum.
My face to be eaten. My bones
To be chewn.
Thum, thum, thum.
My unasked for guest is demanding a feedin'.
Oh! Where's Spaceman Spiff when we really do need
him?
There's something that's lurking right here
In my room.
Thum, thum, thum.

Though I’m wide awake I do not
Move a muscle.
Thum, thum, thum.
It moves 'round my room and I hear
Its soft rustle.
Thum, thum, thum.
Surely it sees me. I lie in my bed
With no other purpose than getting it fed.
There’s something that hungers right here
In my room.
Thum, thum, thum.

Finally, it’s reaching.
I see the Abyss.
Thum, thum, thum.
Incisors are gnashing to
Render Death’s Kiss.
Thum, thum, thum.
I strike at its liver. I gouge at its eyes.
Caught unaware, now it panic it flies.
There’s something that’s trying to flee
From my room.
Thum, thum, thum.

My grip can't be broken. My arms
Are like steel.
Thum, thum, thum.
The Thing sees its ending.
It's starting to squeal.
Thum, thum, thum.
This young whippersnapper disturbing *my* rest?
My own set of fangs sink now deep in its flesh.
It's brought me my dinner right here
To my room.
Thum, thum, thum.

* Too much time spent watching Star Trek - I don't believe in "no win" scenarios.

I Must Be

I know that I'm not perfect
- And that my endless shame
Beyond the sands of all the earth
And all the stars unnamed.

But - yes - I must be better
For I know it is required.
I must take another task
Though long - so long - past tired.

I must take your burdens
Though they are light to heft,
Shoulder all your paltry loads
To give "Poor Atlas" rest.

I must be the one to call.
('Cause your phone doesn't work.)
I must be the adult one.
(For you are such a jerk.)

I must be still water
While you - the typhoon - rage.
I …the Voice of Reason
To your "baboon encaged."

I must offer friendship
While returned a hollow ruse.
Yes, I must be the starlight
To your primordial ooze.

I must be much kinder,
So you may be so cruel.
I must be the wise old sage,
So you may play the Fool.

I must strive for sainthood,
For you? …a lowly cur.
Yes, I must be the god-like being
That your existence slurs.

I know I must be better
For that's what I must do
To put up with those lesser beings,
Those assholes just like you.

*Although we introverts may stay silent, it doesn't mean we like how we're being treated.

The Inky Bird

I followed me
An inky bird
As it flew
And fluttered
To land upon
A silent house
To clasp upon a shutter.

It peeked in through
The window pane
And pecked
Upon the glass.
Inside that room
I knew I'd find
A man who breathed his last.

If the bird
A harbinger
Or a gatherer of souls
...Well, I am just
A mortal man
And am not meant to know.

But beauteous was that
Ebon bird.
I can't
Believe it ill
And know some day
I'll think it fair
To see it on my sill.

* Inspired by a water colour of a bird in flight whose wings threw off a splatter of black droplets.

I Hear Them Calling

I hear them calling,
But I know they'll never find me.
Though they'll search forever,
They could never come so far.
I hear them calling,
But there's something here that binds me,
Turns my answer to a whisper,
A voice inside a jar.

I hear them calling.
They have searched through all the ages,
Sung their songs out to the darkness
In hope someone would hear.
I hear them calling
From a thousand bright lit cages
Through the distances between us
To make it seem more near.

I hear them calling
In the words of my creation,
Lifted toward the heavens
To start their journey home.
Do they hear my answer
Out across the desolation
- In its melody of sadness -
And know they're not alone?

If the universe conspires to bring
"Reunion," how our souls will sing
A joy beyond these mortal things
In which we house our lives.
Until that day - if it should come -
I'll listen to the song above
And pass the tune - like duty - on
And so will I survive.

*To paraphrase Arthur C. Clarke, "...Either we are alone in the universe or we are not. Both are equally..." humbling.

Umbra

Wee Umbra went out wandering
And came upon a jar
All filled with twists of glowing mists
And whirling, dancing stars.

She picked it up and took it home
And put it on her table
- Just the same as I'd have done
If only I'd been able -
And, as it sat there glowing,
It cast such wondrous shadows
Of eagle's claws and toothy maws
And dragons in their battles,
Of moths and birds, and fancy-font words
And rodents with bright swords,
And oodles and oodles of non-descript doodles,
Bound snuggly with old Celtic cords.

The little girl would sit for hours
And drink in every scene,
Absorbing every detail
That her eye could glean.

And every night she'd fall asleep
Amidst the dancing shadows
And walk in dreams of summer streams
Where wizards plied and dabbled.

Then every dawn she'd spring awake
And leap out of her bed,
Not remembering, but still gladdened
By where her dreams had led.
Then off to school, like Momma said,
Where she'd sit there squirming,
Thinking of the little jar
With all its shadows churning.

But, coming home from school one day,
Her tabletop was bare
Except for her pet kitty cat
Who slept without a care.

"Montague! What have you done!?"
Yelled the little Miss.
But Monty merely cracked one eye
And made his tail go "swish."

And then she spied - and nearly cried -
Her jar upon the floor,
Whole, intact, but lid uncapped
And emptied of its lore.

No screams, no sobs, no tearful daubs,
The girl just stood struck dumb
And all that night spoke not a word,
Not a sound - not one!
Until at last 'twas time for bed.
She crawled into her sheets
And fell into a silent place
Of dark and dreamless sleep.

As Umbra slept, a spider swept
Its web of dust and dirt
And came upon two shiny things
So bright its eight eyes hurt.

Two small stars had fled the jar
Only to snag in the web
Where they danced and they glowed right above
Umbra's nose
Only three feet from her head.

They were stuck and entrapped, so the spider enwrapped
The stars in a fine silken cord,
But, no matter how spindled, their bright light rekindled
And stabbed at its eyes like a sword.

So the spider then clipped and carefully snipped
The thread that had bound the two stars
And they fell like a shot 'til the two glowing dots
Came to rest on the sleeping girl's arm.

But even from there, they gave off a glare
That the spider just couldn't ignore,
So, hand over hand - over hand, over hand -
Downward it went to explore
'Til it came the tundra, the hide of Great Umbra,
Upon which the burning motes lay.
The stars shook with fear as the spider drew near
And flared up as bright as the day.

But no harm did it do to the sharp pointed two.
It just scooped them right up like their nanny,
Then looked all around 'til finally it found
A place that was shady - and handy.

Then here's what it did - it lifted the lid
Of each of Umbra's great eyes
And, into each one, it placed a wee sun,
Then back to its web it did climb.

Early next morning, when she was done snoring,
Umbra fair leapt from her bed
To land on the floor, then rush out the door,
A million bright scenes in her head.

She babbled and burbled and nearly turned purple,
So eager to tell all her tales
That few notarized the new lights in her eyes
That glowed from within without fail.

And still to this day, there the stars stay
To lumen her eyes in rich amber.
And she still loves to chat about this and 'bout that
And her dreamings that each night still clamour.

And when she's not jawing, she's sitting there drawing
Such marvelous magical scenes
- From glowing green cats to sad swordsman rats,
Shiny, brave knights and their Queens.

There’re hybridized bats and new Zodiacs
And doggies with tails all a-waggin’,
And black, inky things with splattered-on wings,
And even a non-'ffensive dragon.

All of these things, to her nightly bring
The stars that still dwell in her eyes
And then every day she shares what she may
With ink and with paper reprised.

There’s no way of stemming the scenes never ending,
So she draws them to make room for more.
For if she does not, she fears the whole lot
Will blow up and burst out the door.

Then where would she be, poor little-girl wee,
With nothing but stars in her eyes?
So she vents all the pressures by drawing her treasures
To give us small glimpses inside.

*She knows who she is.

Butterflies 2

Memories, like butterflies,
I watch them as they flutter by,
Flash their colours 'cross my eyes,
Upon my cheek their kiss.

Footprints on the sands of time,
In butterflies have I left mine.
A silent song within the rhyme.
No better life than this.

*This was deemed "a little sad" by my beta reader. ...Maybe, but to me, that was hidden by the piece's warmth.

www.ingramcontent.com/pod-product-compliance
Lightning Source LLC
Chambersburg PA
CBHW020908080526
44589CB00011B/494